Into the Ruins

Into the Ruins

Poems

Frederick Glaysher

Earthrise Press

Grateful acknowledgment is made to the editors of *Chaminade Literary Review,* "Basic Training," "The Crowned Maitreya"; and *Empyrea,* "Elegy for Robert Hayden"; to the Fulbright Commission for a grant in 1994 to China, where some of these poems were either written or revised; and to the National Endowment for the Humanities for a Summer Seminar in 1995 on South Asia, making possible one of the poems on India. My published essays and reviews are available on my website at http://members.tripod.com/~fglaysher/index.htm

Publisher's Cataloging-in-Publication
(Provided by Quality Books, Inc.)

Glaysher, Frederick, 1954-
        Into the Ruins : Poems / Frederick Glaysher. —
    1st ed.
        p. cm.
        LCCN: 99-60972
        ISBN: 0-9670421-2-7
        1. Postmodernism—Poetry. 2. War poetry, American. I. Title.
    PS3557.L37I62 1999   811'.54
                        QBI99-522

Earthrise Press
P. O. Box 81842, Rochester, MI 48308-1842

For Pamela

Contents

Preface

During the last two hundred years poetry has undergone a steadily increasing submersion in the self. The romantics turned from rationality and the community of interest to aestheticism and private phantasmagorias. They reveled in the sensitivities of the mind, what Matthew Arnold called the "dialogue of the mind with itself." The Victorians contracted the subjective disease and lingered through the rest of the century. The modernists affected a radical departure from romanticism but soon proved a different strain of the same malaise. The disease worsened, the isolation increased, the outlook narrowed. The postmodernists resigned themselves to their own little personal worlds.

William Wordsworth's admonition that "poets do not write for poets alone but for men" has come to seem a reprimand or cruel joke. History has not stopped to wonder why. Throughout the last few hundred years, many oppressive monarchies and regimes have been cast aside; antiquated institutions have been discredited and left behind; peoples have striven for and won greater affirmation of human rights. The cost has been incalculable, the waste immense. Two world wars swept over the globe, caused untold agony and hardship, extinguished the lives of at least sixty-five million individual human beings. Communism augmented the horror by murdering tens of millions of people, while the West suffered in its own way. Amidst such a wasteland of a century, such carnage and confusion, poetry could find no rhyme or reason.

Now at the end of the twentieth century, far from withdrawing further into the self and into an obfuscating use of language, poets must turn to viewing and contemplating the real world, where men butcher and kill, love and hate, aspire and sometimes achieve. For out of our experience and contemplation of the past and present, a deeper understanding of history and of what it means to be a human being is now beginning to emerge, opening the way to a new future, in a new century. W. H. Auden once wrote that radical change in artistic style is contingent on "radical change in human sensibility." The unrelenting movement of modern times toward the oneness of humankind has sufficiently been made explicit—an epic movement that allows, produces, and requires a fundamental change in sensibility.

". . . and so man constructs poetry out of the remnants found in ruins."

Czeslaw Milosz

I

The Sleep of Reason Produces Monsters
(Goya)

Bent over his desk he sleeps,
head buried in his arms,
trying to shut out the creatures
of the night, the screeching bats
and owls that throng about him,
alight on his desk, offer him a pen
to sketch visions of horror,
as two gleaming-eyed cats,
one about to pounce, look on and grrr.

Midnight Visitors

Mainly indistinct faces circling
in front of me in the abyss of night,
but at times I see a Cambodian
next to a neatly stacked pile of skulls,
a Jew staring from a crack in a boxcar,
an African, more corpse than man,
faltering through a desert that is as
desiccated as the landscape of our soul.

The Pit of Darkness

Night descends. The almost inaudible groans
of suffering begin to be heard again.
O damned darkness, what new horror
do you hold in your hand?

I clamber from the futon, fall, crawl
along the floor, groping for the door,
for some way to escape the inescapable terror
of the reality I cannot bear.

But the next room too is a black pit
filled with all-pervading darkness,
and the next, and the next, and the next
are all like the torture-chambers of this world.

Danse Macabre
(for Baga)

Three a.m. Specters invade my brain
wrenching me from sleep as violently
as those tender ones in Assam were wrenched
from life.

I think of friends growing up in India
with dirt blowing in through crevices
in the walls, waking them up
at night.

Then the wall of my own room fades away
and the dead drag themselves past me
from Iran, South Africa, Lebanon.

Locusts

I
Torn from a dream,
I hear them in the trees,
rise from bed,
stand a moment at the window
looking into the blackness of the night.

I turn and think of refugees
in Virginia, hacking out a farm
so far from Laos.

"Someday they'll call themselves Virginians."

II
Down a dark hall I walk
and reach a room shadowed
as though it were occluded
with the lies of our Myth.

"Free at last, free at last,
thank God Almighty, I'm free at last."

Eternal words written for an eternal world.

Camp II
(Poston, Arizona)

Across the floating bridge of dreams,
the scorching Hell of people choking on dust,
caged like rats behind miles of wire,
miles of that damned fence—
machine guns in guard towers,
floodlights searching for the schemes of Tokyo.

Like a bad dream it goes by,
tar paper roofs blown off in the night,
a place beyond description and tears.

Gulag Wayfarers

Through darkness they come,
through sub-zero nights,
through snow and taiga,
the shades of the fallen,
their columns driven along by dogs,
their hair and clothing covered with ice.

Around me they gather and moan.
"Speak. Speak for those who are dead."

Oracle Bones

T'ien forgotten, a century of convulsion;
democracy, a goddess of mercy engulfed;
a roll soaked in human blood, no medicine;
all the Long Marches leading nowhere;
one Great Leap Forward, six feet under;
Hundreds of withered Flowers strewn before
the grave of a decade of disaster.

Cawing, a crow rises from a severed branch,
flaps heavily toward the horizon.

Heartland America
(for Bill)

Out of the late twentieth century,
the victims of violence,
crawling, dragging themselves forward,
nails digging into the earth,
pulling along decapitated bodies,
exposing sliced throats,
bullet wounds gaping in heads and chests,
mourn, for a nation lost,
in a cannibal nihilism that knows no bottom.

II

Into the Ruins
(for Kozo)

I

Smoke curls above the ruins of Lebanon
that smother the bodies of those
who had hoped for peace.

Behind broken walls broken men and women
seek refuge from a fury that stalks them
as relentlessly as destiny.

I lie in bed looking into the dark
and see nothing but the vaguest fancies
mankind has ever dreamt.

Somewhere behind a broken wall
something begins to move, to assume
a shape met somewhere once before.

Out from the ruins he steps and stands
amid the scintillating dark,
waiting quietly.

II

Fire and smoke and another street
in another time. The Black Sea
and the blackness of Trebizond.

Churches burning. Houses seized.
Women married to their children's murderers.
And the marching of hundreds of thousands

to their death in the desert.
Stabbed along the road. Shot in the back.
Dragged into the hills and raped to death.

Kicked from a bridge into the Euphrates,
none finding it good to cross over,
all dying of hunger and thirst in Aleppo.

From the shadows we watch the efficiency
of the formidable modern state,
of the Committee of Union and Progress.

III

Coiling, swirling, swaying above our heads,
smoke and the stench of human flesh
burst from the hellhole of Auschwitz.

In the ghastly glow the demons weave
their macabre and haunting dance
around the flaming pit.

And like horrible gigantic flares
every chimney in the yard vomits fire
tainted with human ash.

Through the fence of the crematory
we watch leaping figures,
silhouettes against the flames,

turn corpses with pitchforks,
pour fuel on people who still writhe
with the pain of life.

IV
Eight fifteen. A clear day transmogrified
into an inferno,
into smoke and ash.

Along the road he stands,
his eyeball in his hand,
gazing in horror.

And everywhere we walk
others struggle and squirm and shudder,
arms bent forward,

skin blackened and peeling from their bones,
kimono patterns burnt deep
into their flesh—

human specters of human wrong—
everywhere everywhere everywhere
nightmare people staggering in darkness.

V

Seen through smoke,
past five-month-old rotting bodies,
Muslim militiamen brandish from a jeep

jawless Christian skulls on cudgels,
wave them with glee to taunt those
who butchered old women and children

now dried to ash by the Lebanese sun.
We move past withered remains
and out of the broken building.

And those sockets that once knew life,
that saw the One Sun rise and set,
rise and set, stare back.

I stumble down the hill
as one lost in blindness
stumbles through darkness.

Old Baltimore

All night long dreams of horror filled my mind,
images of old men hanged from trees,
women raped with brutal bestiality.

Outside my window in the morning light
eight-year-old paperboys bickered and cursed.
"You black! You black old woman!"

Rodin's *Gates of Hell*

I
Ueno Park

In the heart of Tokyo, Ueno Park blooms
in cherry blossoms, vibrant, lush,
refuge for millions in need of room
to breathe, to think, to watch
their children walking in the shade.

We come too in search of peace, of beauty,
found only in public places, where men and women,
young and old, stroll for the sheer glory
of the joy of life, for the rich diversity
of people freed for the day from strife.

II
At the National Museum of Western Art

"RELINQUISH ALL HOPE, YE WHO ENTER HERE"
cleaves time asunder, wrenches me from dreams,
as once in Detroit Rodin's *Gates of Hell*
loomed up before me, dread commentary
on all that waste and agony that swarms
beyond the pilasters of that portal,
opens onto the threshold of our century,
our deathbed, childbed age,
glutted with deep and unacknowledged darkness.

So here in Ueno Park, unknown, unexpected,
the *Gates* open onto a closed country,
terrifying image of Japan, of France,
of the United States and all the West,
whose multitudes in distracted turmoil
writhe in the searing inferno
of passion, hatred, skulduggery,
wailing, shrieking, blown about by the wind
that rages through the halls of horror.

III
The Thinker

Staring into the portal I see humankind
stretched out on the rack of this century,
gassed in the trenches of Europe,
vivisected in the meat shops of Germany,
forced to kowtow in China and India,
in Africa and the archipelagoes,
by the British, the French, the Japanese,
by all those intent on empire,
intent on the worship of themselves.

Staring into the portal I see ourselves
revealed in the terror of what we are,
of what we cannot face, cannot bear,
try always to ignore,
while the cost grows greater and greater,
while like Ugolino we grope over the dead,
the victims of our rapacity,
our devouring lust.
"O Master, the sense is hard."

Hibakusha Nightmare

O image I cannot forget,
scar-fried corpse in the midst of flight
cradling a charred infant
from the horrible, hot light.

Advent of the Beast

I stand on the sand of the sea
and a great beast rises up,
half lion, half bear,
head of a man frothing at the mouth,
seeking prey, tossing its horns about.
Oh what rough beast is this?
So many centuries to end in nightmare.

Down, down, down, down it swoops
on those who wonder after it,
tearing their bones apart,
sucking out their blood and marrow,
exulting in its power,
its stolen seat of authority,
its image that blasphemes the stars above.

Raskolnikov's Dream

In delirium, I see the plague,
microbes sweeping across Europe,
infecting the souls of men,
replacing all with a strange new certainty,
a madness claiming infallible
its decisions, scientific conclusions,
morals that mock the word.

Man falls on man,
towns and villages rage,
nations erupt in frenzy,
no one understands anyone,
none can judge or agree,
"all that's solid melts into air,
all that's holy is profaned."

"Of ancient Europe
remains but a shred,"
fathomless blood blots out the rest,
horror unmentionable,
darkness impenetrable,
violence and famine,
destruction and war.

To the New City
(A.D. 430)

Dearest Paulinus,
    I grieve that I do not see you,
but I take comfort that we have always
been united in the service of Christ
and His Heavenly City. During the last
several weeks I've often thought
what blessed lives we've had.
    I trust you've heard the Vandals have
overrun Numidia, laying waste to everything.
Just yesterday word came of another atrocity.
The second bishop this month was stripped,
tortured, and murdered outside his town.
Whole cities have been pillaged and hundreds
of villas razed. Even more refugees
have been flocking into Hippo than after
the sack of Rome, so many years ago.
The people, I'm afraid, weak as ever, are
in the throes of despair. The clergy,
holy virgins, and ascetics have dispersed.
Many, heedless of their vows, desert
at the slightest sign of peril.
It pains me deeply that dozens of churches
have been burnt and the divine sacraments
left either unsought or unadministered
for lack of priests. Again it is the time
of the pressing of the olive oil.
Through these massacres, fires, and lootings,
sick men may yet seek the grace of Christ,
the spirit turn to clear flowing oil.

27

So it was after Rome was sacked, and,
God willing, these latest adversities
will lead the people to His throne.
Remember, after the scourge of Alaric,
I averred Rome was punished but not replaced.
My, how long it's been since I thought that.
Recently I exhorted the brethren
not to lose heart, for there will be an end
to every earthly kingdom. What Christian
bends the knee and this does not believe?
If it is the end now, God sees.
Perhaps it has not yet come to that.
For some reason we are hoping, in our
frailty, it has not come to that.
And so I attend to the present and
look to the future. That sweet city will
descend, regardless of all upheavals.
We must not refuse to regain our youth
in Christ. An odd report has reached me.
The Vandals are cutting down olive trees
throughout the land.

    I fear I may not write again,
what with the siege and a touch of fever.
Know that as always my prayers beseech
Christ for your abiding health, my friend.
How fondly I recall your views that
Christian friendships are made in heaven,
predestined by God. Surely ours has been
such a bond.

    Farewell until we bow together before
His throne. In His Name,
Augustine

Long Journey Through Night
(O'Neill)

Mind shattered, Mary paces the floor,
paces the floor, drifts outside
along the veranda with her hair
streaming in the midnight air,
flowing over her shoulders
in the dark light that shows her
more than she can ever tell.

Like a phantasm she glides along in
dainty slippers, clothed in a sky-blue
dressing gown covered with embroideries,
face pale, eyes enormous and glistening
like polished black jewels,
over one arm her old wedding gown
trailing on the floor.

Night after night she's haunted by
the memory of her lost bridegroom:
Oh will he not come again!
No, no, no, he's dead.
Go, go to thy deathbed.
He will never come again.
He's gone. He's gone.

The Crowned Maitreya

Early we rise and make our way
across the congested teeming city
to the front main gate, entangled
in electrical cables for the trains,
walk unchallenged past the clay
statues of the guardians of Buddhism.

The walls shun the noise of the traffic.
Sweet coolness pervades the morning air.
Here in the old capital of peace,
we seek out this place of peace, Koryu-ji,
temple of the Hata families after their
long journey from China and Korea.

The monks have finished their morning prayers,
abandoned the temple and lecture hall
to the daily influx of tourists.
An old man sweeps stray leaves and sticks
from bare ground and sprinkles water
on the flagstone path.

We wait patiently while these rituals
are performed and talk of Shotoku's hall,
his Code of Laws, his love of peace
and harmony, of the great service
he rendered Koryu-ji and Japan.
Such a ruler hasn't appeared in centuries.

The bronze door of the museum opens,
we pay a pittance, walk in,
skirt along the rigid lifeless icons.
We know what we have come to see.
In the placid morning we stand,
oblivious of time, enraptured by his beauty.

Suddenly they arrive bellowing,
cackling, trampling the silence.
We step back and let them rush by,
their guide swinging a pennon,
Nikons and Canons frantically clicking,
their national treasure captured for posterity.

Off to one side the old attendant
watches from his post at the door.
We wait for echoes to fade away.
He shambles to the altar, rings a graceful
bell three times, offers a prayer
we all acknowledge with a bow.

Carnelian Blemish

Five years old and writhing
in a street of Assam,

his stomach slashed open,
hot entrails hanging from him,

the stain spreading
around him on the ground,

while flies cover his still-alive
and quivering guts.

Leader of the People

Gentlemen, we've got to do something.
If we don't act now, we may lose our chance.
We know what's best for our country
and must protect its vital interests.
We must act now before our sovereign right
to wage war is abrogated
by these deluded one-worlders.
We have the political realism to see
mankind can never live peaceably
under a global federation.
The nation-states have been locked in
vehement hatred and distrust
for too long for such a thing to occur.
And then there's the insurmountable
problem of cultural differences.
It's bewildering to think of
the primitive peoples, languages,
customs, religions, philosophies
that separate and mar the societies of
our foreign friends and neighbors.
If we can somehow beef up our borders,
reinculcate that passionate devotion
to God and country that once made us
so great, I'm sure we'll put a halt
to this sentimental drift.
And that's why I called you here today.
We must uncover the utopian fantasy
of the so-called United Nations
and stop wasting so much money on it.

It's no longer enough to depend on
man's natural xenophobia to hamstring
its efforts; nor can we rely any longer
on the inadequacies of its constitution.
(Need I remind you of the alarming
tendency to override our wishes?)
No, before it is too late, we must
strike a decisive blow. If we delay,
I'm convinced we'll ultimately regret it.

Vignette

The ovens burned twenty-four hours a day
for so long the bricks glowed;
more than smoke went up those chimneys.

Chairman of the Board

No, I don't mind talking to you.
Being supervisor of this here county,
folks naturally want to know what
I think. And I always tell 'em.
Take pride in that fact, I do.
Well now, I've been elected for
twenty-eight years running and expect
to keep right on being elected.
Folks in these parts know I serve 'em well,
so when election time comes round
there's never hardly no question
about who they're gunna vote for.
This year ain't no exception.
Of course I always go out and talk to 'em
right at their door, and don't treat
the colored people no different.
Twenty-eight years ago I went to their
front door and told 'em straight,
and this year I'll do it again.
They understand. We get along real good.
When they come in here to my store,
I talk to 'em just like ever'body else,
and their money is as good as anybody's.
Look, my door's not closed to 'em.
And you won't find no business in all
of Quitan County that shuts 'em out.
Let me put it this way,
I ain't gunna eat or sleep with 'em,
not in a thousand years,

but we can all just get along.
No reason to rock the boat.
They got their lives, and we got ours,
and that's the way it's always been.
As county supervisor I have
their best interests in mind.
Just the other day me and the Board
were discussing what to do about
Hadleyburg. (That's at the other end
of the county, near Alabama.)
Problem over there is people don't know
no better than to let the swamp water
come right up round the house.
Makes for an awful damn stink.
Don't help with the skeeters either,
not to mention a few other problems.
Well, like I say, we're thinking hard
about what to do. If we only had
a real tax base over there we could put in
a drainpipe or two and take care
of the problem in nothing flat.
Trouble is though, if you have ten people
and only one job, you're gunna have
nine outa work. It don't matter
what race they are, whether they're colored
or white. We keep trying to get
industry to move into the county.
It ain't easy being supervisor and
always having to worry about these things,
but I think we're making progress.

At a Mass Grave

I
Gelid eyeballs gawk at nothing.
Arms and legs twist together.
Lifeless jaws gape in horror.
Livid torsos caress no more.

II
Boys and girls, men and women,
too young to walk, too weak to stand,
dumped into a ditch
like trash into a garbage can.

Wild Goose Pagodas

The sounds of traffic ascend from Xi'an
reaching me on the hotel balcony six floors up.
So Wang Wei once listened to the pagoda bell,
awakened from his dreams to the day's demands,
while Tu Fu climbed the many stairs,
finding peace in acceptance of his lot.

Suffering is nothing new to humankind.
Yet I can never leave it at that.
Who can fail to feel the pain of a human face?

III

A Conversation on the Forum

Juvenal. How can one stomach
this unambitious bunch braying
about the self in unbearable bromides?
They make me want to puke.
Persius. Though considerably more detached,
I understand the sentiment.
May I advise a more Stoic tone,
one that proceeds with greater control?
Juv. You're urging me to be as sycophantic
as they? These minor birds think only about
the promotion of their reputations.
All that matters to them is appearing
at the right time in the right place
with literati who glitter in the glare of Nothing.
They are all noise and empty sound,
a storm of words with little sense.
Prompted by a herd of academicians,
who exploit their formalistic verse,
they strut and bleat to the acclamation
of their epigones. For anointed
dullness they outrank even Shadwell
and Cibber. Damn, what drivel.
Per. I too have thought and said as much.
The verse in vogue is smooth and equal,
befitting those who have their eye more
on their career than on the thing itself.
Doggerel stuff. Were any manly
virtue left in Rome, no one would
tolerate such servile versifiers.

Juv. We need tragic satires and epics.
"Arma virumque cano."
Per. Even to allude to him seems absurd.
He was truly great and looked outside
himself at the saga of history,
at Rome's long odyssey from the time
ships first sailed for our land
to the crowning glory of Augustus.
These petty birds masturbate their minds.
But why turn from self to horror?
Juv. Listen carefully and I'll tell you
the causes that have led my Muse:
When murderers routinely butcher innocents
with impunity, claim insanity
and shortly walk the streets
to perpetrate another heinous crime;
when burglars plunder citizens' estates
only to be slapped on the wrist
and released on farcical probation,
some cozening their parole officers
into helping them to rob again;
when our jails train thieves to commit
crimes from their own prison cells,
aided by accomplices on the "outside";
when society is raped of all moral standards,
can neither convincingly refute
the anti-values of common thugs or dictators,
but worships money above all else,
and breeds a facile mentality evidenced alike

44

by crooks, lawyers, and lying emperors;
when the poor are denied a meager dole,
while gambling becomes a national pastime
used to finance what passes for education,
and our wise forefathers are forgotten,
then it's hard to write, but harder to forbear,
to view so base a world and to refrain.
For what age cultivated so much vice,
or when was avarice so pervasive?
What indignation smoulders in my brain
when more babies are clinically dispatched
than ever were exposed on Grecian mountains,
buried beneath Arabian sands,
or flung into Chinese rivers.
How can we have the gall to prattle
about rights while we take them away
on such a massive scale, and oh so
scientifically? Now one can rent
a surrogate womb for a few aurei,
even a virgin if one can be found.
How have we lost all human feeling?
Do you defend our degenerate times?
Per. No. All balance has been lost.
Moral sense and vocabulary are
leaching out of our lives and language.
Messalina begins to look virtuous.
Juv. Are men any better?
Per. Of course not. More pathetic than ever.
In our vast cities debauchery

has never been so systematically
promoted, advertised, inculcated.
Still I fear you strike too fiercely
with satire's rod. Mollify a little.
Juv. I'll not stand by and watch my country ruined.
So I say, satire, spread thy sails,
survey the horrors of this century,
balk before no atrocity, probe all
the damnable deeds that lay bare
the festering heart at this juncture.
Listen to the clamorous bars,
full of drunkards and drug addicts,
hear the screaming sirens that blare
across the cities of our land,
sift through the rubble of war,
find the corpses and wrap them
in a humane and pitying embrace.

Mud-Wrestlers

The mud-wrestlers struggle
in the continuous flow
of feculent ooze that streams
from the mushy mudhole.

All they understand is their long years
of bathing in swill,
of rubbing the chalky-gray sludge
into each other's head.

Only what's inside the sloshy arena
matters to them, only the slough exists,
perceived by innumerable
clods of clay.

And the crowd just loves it,
cheers each soiled participant
on and on and on,
from their safe, ringside seats.

Derrida in Doubt

Like a gargoyle perched on the corner
of a prison-house, he gurgles
his charismatic discourse, plays freely
with risks found at that misty height,
affirms and erases the logocentricism
that webs together all and Nothing.

Turned toward a formalistic labyrinth,
toward innovation's specious lure,
a strange nonpresence becomes present,
denies but seeks not to destroy
the world, the author and his works,
his words, his notions that repress.

The Looking-Glass

*"When man has withdrawn into the quick-
silver at the back of the mirror no great
event becomes luminous in his mind."*
                              Yeats

Self: Stand by my side and look into the mirror
with me. There we'll see the touchstone
of all reality and truth;
there we'll perceive the image of ourselves,
the retreat of immediacy,
the interior cave fashioned by Descartes.

Poet: No, I will carry it through the streets,
render an image of every created thing.
I will turn it round and round
so that everyone can see
the sun, the stars, the sky,
the appearance of the horror of reality.

Self: Your horror is but an activity of
your mind—if it's truth you want,
look to sensation that streams within you,
simultaneously enveloping everything
in a deluge of flux that blazons
the truth you cannot face.

Poet: Truth! What do you know of truth,
you who warp nature and smile,
pampering your personality.
I'm sick of your ugly face in the mirror.

I'll do what you're too effete to do.
I'll admit the odious facts.

Self: I've done that by looking into the mirror,
expressing genuinely what I found there.
Your problem is you lack sincere feeling,
have archaic conceptions of the correspondence
between word and meaning,
between time and space.

Poet: Your conceptions are empty and criminal.
You take yourself as subject and expect
others to listen—how vain!
What action have you ever imitated?
What deed have you ever admired?
I'll make my stand on the given world,

and on that beauty that draws us forward,
even in childhood, into harmony
with the splendor of reason,
the splendor of the essential forms.
And I'll delight by teaching that justice
without which all is lost.

IV

Elijah Lovejoy

The cry, the cry of the oppressed,
has reached not only my ears
but pierced my very soul,
and as long as I live,
I will not hold my peace.

Eleanor Roosevelt

Thousands wrote, amended, quibbled
over wording and content,
upheld the traditions of East and West,
of Aquinas and Confucius,
defended individual and social rights.

She was not alone, but she alone had
the vision, the drive, the determination
to create, out of lesser loyalties,
the Universal Declaration of Human Rights,
the Magna Carta of all mankind.

Albert Einstein

Because he changed our thinking
he knew our thinking has to change
from stopping at national borders
to a new kind of loyalty,
holding relative
the bellicose dimension of hatred
extending throughout the continuum of time,
given a mass beyond its due.

Though ridiculed and heckled, he gauged
the pressure of the fear the jingoes
misjudged with their outdated thinking.
And when his efforts prove not to have
been in vain, all humankind will admire
the earthly shape of his wisdom.

Dag Hammarskjöld

No more of these sad tones
of fear and the scourge of war,
of chaos and anarchy,
of the passions of humankind.

Though the first movements wander
among the dark and threatening
conflicts of Beethoven's *Ninth*,
the "Ode to Joy" shall come.

All the millions will unite
as brothers, surrendered
to the way of peace,
to a higher synthesis of joy.

Homage to Mark Tobey

nastaliq
    hiragana
        kanji
  living
   lines
     of
       calligraphy
intertwining
    in
      space
        in
          time
  word
    beyond
    time
      beyond
       space

mass
  of
    rhythm
      of
        music
  vibrating
    moving
      dancing
brush
  strokes
    shimmering
  tension
    of
      depth
        of
          equilibrium

transparent
        tracery
  ethereal
        white
                tablets
  invocations
                inundating
                        renewing
  pouring
        down
                on
                  one
                    world

Elegy for Robert Hayden

Blue jays scream in the trees.
Winter's late snow begins to fall.
All nature seems to grieve for you.
Yet I know it is only I,
I and others who also disbelieve
the feared and all-too-sudden change
that has left us with nothing but
delayed and swirling gusts of winter snow.
And even they will soon be gone.

V

To Penelope

And so the gods gave me my homecoming,
and we are together again in our own bed.
Oh to lie here with you after so many years
of war, of trial, of wandering and suffering!

What bliss to hold you in my arms,
to feel your deep kisses and bare breasts on mine,
to wrap our legs together after twenty long years!
O Penelope! Thank the gods we're together again!

For twenty years I savored the memories
of the wild nights and summer of our youth.
They were nothing compared to this sweet night,
after many hard years of faithfulness and love.

Intimations
(for Elliot)

In the early morning light,
the sun having shed its crimson
for luxuriant golden rays
that heighten the clouds of glory,

we watch our child eating breakfast,
humming, frolicking with his spoon,
dangling his feet that reach only
partway from the chair to the floor.

Kagi

Half way to Tokyo in a little side-station,
I sit down to await the next train.
From around a corner of the building
a six-year-old boy hastens up to me,
asks in his childish voice for help.
I follow him to a wornout bicycle,
his mother gasping as I approach, smile,
kneel to inspect the key and front-wheel lock.
The boy crouches to look intently with me.
I jiggle and bang the bent and stuck key
until it snaps free. We all cheer.
Thanking me the woman whisks him into
the carrier. I assure her it was nothing.
As the mother pedals off, the child,
hair tousled, turns round smiling
and waves and waves and waves.

Basic Training

At last I was going to get
to meet Uncle Benny, who lost
a leg in World War II.

I dashed up Grandma's stairs
clutching a surplus canteen,
showed him I had one too.

Laughing he taught me how
to put it on and dandled me
on his wooden knee.

A Visit to Aunt Amy's

Aunt Amy wanted me to visit,
and I knew it would be special.
She lived with the veterans
of foreign wars. Men on crutches
smoked propped against the building,
greeted her as she led me along,
past them and the basket men,
some with their stumps unshrouded,
roasting in the morning sun.
As we walked through the lobby,
a man without legs, strapped on
a dolly, rolled by happily barking,
"G'morning Amy. Nice day ain't it?"

Leaving the Old Country

Cursing the wars of Mitteleuropa,
Great-grandpa Vugrinec got demobbed from
the Hapsburg army, sold the family store,
bribed his way out of Croatia,
hurried through the gates of Ellis Island.

The Dream

Man is darkness, the stranger said.
I wanted to say man is light.

His motives are base beyond belief.
He can rise to selfless nobility.

His lusts are never satisfied.
He can deny, withhold himself.

Violence is his daily bread.
He can choose to feast at other tables.

His treachery knows no bounds.
He can set them if he wishes.

Man is slime crawled off a rock.
Man is all these things and more.

The Dark Wood

At the end of the century,
midway the journey of my life,
this too is the wind's home,
late in the night,
blowing through empty rooms,
hope of ascent all but lost.

Chamber Music
(in the Black Pit)

He stands in the dark
waiting to hear his name
from the door of the cell.

Vermin wiggle and scurry
through filth on the floor.
Lungs gag on mephitic air.

Everywhere only the touch
of dank, granitic blocks
hewed ages and ages ago.

O interminable bondage,
O cursed incarceration.
Let the gallows call.